FREEDOM'S PROMISE

THE GREAT
MIGRATION

BY DUCHESS HARRIS, JD, PHD
WITH KATE CONLEY

Core Library

An Imprint of Abdo Publishing
abdobooks.com

Cover image: Many African American families fled the
South in the early 1900s.

abdocorelibrary.com

Published by Abdo Publishing, a division of ABDO, PO Box 398166, Minneapolis, Minnesota 55439. Copyright © 2020 by Abdo Consulting Group, Inc. International copyrights reserved in all countries. No part of this book may be reproduced in any form without written permission from the publisher. Core Library™ is a trademark and logo of Abdo Publishing.

Printed in the United States of America, North Mankato, Minnesota
032019
092019

THIS BOOK CONTAINS RECYCLED MATERIALS

Cover Photo: MPI/Archive Photos/Getty Images
Interior Photos: MPI/Archive Photos/Getty Images, 1; Chicago History Museum/Archive Photos/ Getty Images, 5; Everett Historical/Shutterstock Images, 6–7, 14–15, 18, 20, 43; Jun Fujita/ Chicago History Museum/Archive Photos/Getty Images, 9; Red Line Editorial, 12, 27; Oakley Chemical Co./Library of Congress, 22; Bettmann/Getty Images, 24–25; Stan Wayman/The LIFE Picture Collection/Getty Images, 29; Edwin Rosskam/US FSA/OWI/Library of Congress, 31; Mandel Ngan/AFP/Getty Images, 34–35; Fred Stein/picture-alliance/dpa/AP Images, 38; Douglas Graham/ Roll Call/Newscom, 40

Editor: Maddie Spalding
Series Designer: Claire Vanden Branden

Library of Congress Control Number: 2018966046

Publisher's Cataloging-in-Publication Data

Names: Harris, Duchess, author | Conley, Kate, author.
Title: The great migration / by Duchess Harris and Kate Conley
Description: Minneapolis, Minnesota: Abdo Publishing, 2020 | Series: Freedom's promise | Includes online resources and index.
Identifiers: ISBN 9781532118746 (lib. bdg.) | ISBN 9781532172922 (ebook)
Subjects: LCSH: Migration, Internal--United States--History--20th century--Juvenile literature. | Rural-urban migration--United States--Juvenile literature. | African Americans--Social conditions--Juvenile literature. | Blacks--Relocation--Juvenile literature.
Classification: DDC 973.0496--dc23

CONTENTS

A LETTER FROM DUCHESS

Beginning in the early 1900s, Black people began to leave the South in large numbers. This mass movement is known as the Great Migration. Black people wanted to escape violence and discrimination in the South. Many moved to northern cities. But they still encountered discrimination. Many could not find good housing. They were forced to work difficult, low-paying jobs.

Despite these hardships, Black migrants made a place for themselves. They created music and art that became widely popular. Black politicians and activists worked for equal rights. Author Isabel Wilkerson argues that the Great Migration was the first big step that African Americans took without asking. This is a powerful concept.

I had never thought of the Great Migration as an act of political resistance. But the movement of Black people collectively voicing their opposition to the South was indeed a political act. Join me in learning about the history and legacy of the Great Migration. Follow me on a journey that explores the promise of freedom.

Duchess Harris

A family arrives in Chicago in the early 1900s as part of the
Great Migration.

CHAPTER ONE

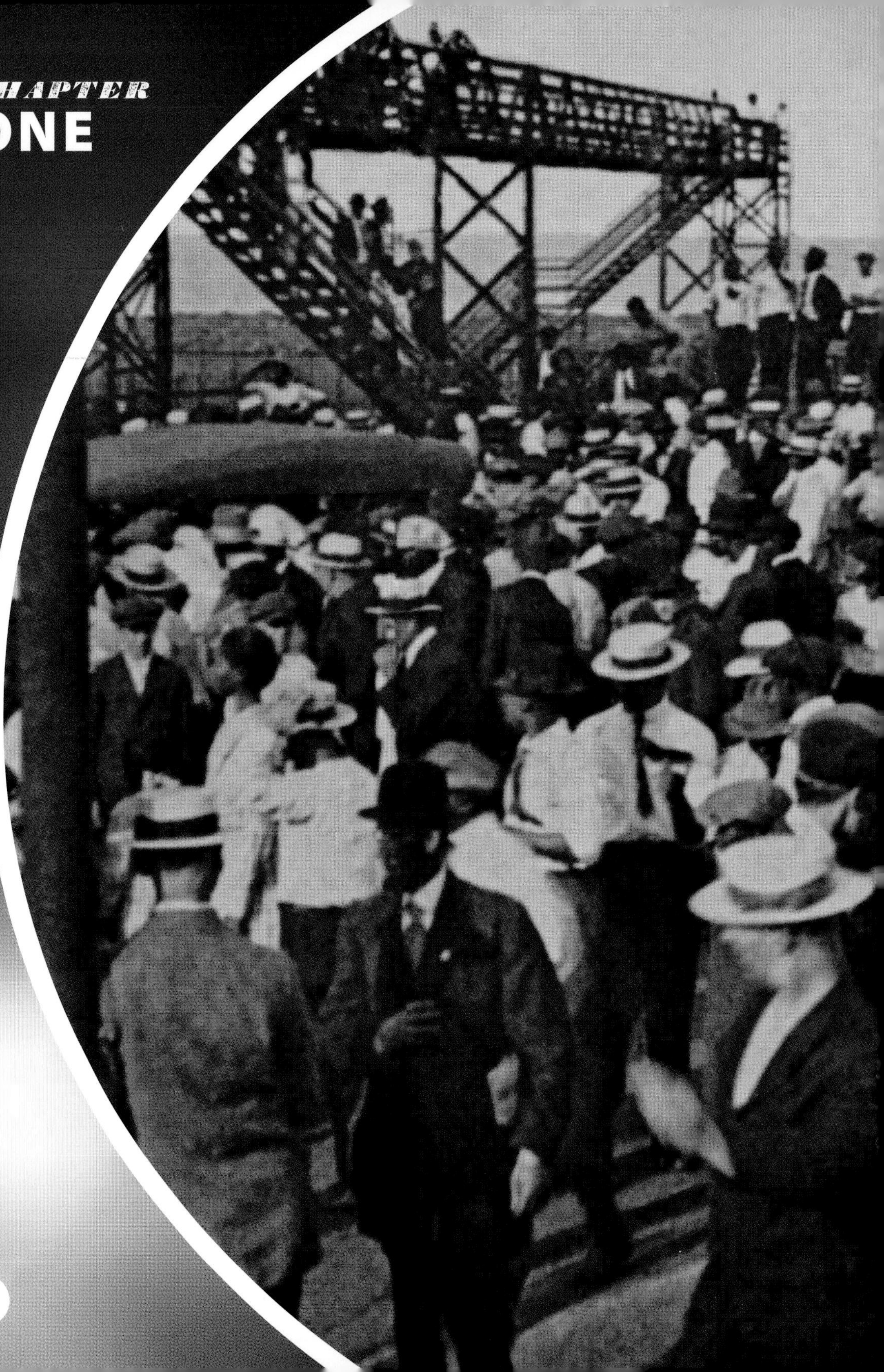

A RIOT ERUPTS

On July 27, 1919, temperatures soared above 90 degrees Fahrenheit (32°C) in Chicago, Illinois. Seventeen-year-old Eugene Williams and his three friends wanted to cool down. They headed for a beach along the shores of Lake Michigan. The teens splashed in the water and then climbed onto a homemade raft.

As the teens floated, the raft drifted across an invisible line. White swimmers stayed on one side of the line. Black swimmers remained on the other side. Williams and his friends were African American. They had floated into the white swimming area. Tensions between white and black people had been simmering

Bystanders leave the Lake Michigan beach in Chicago, Illinois, as the 1919 riot begins.

RACIAL TENSIONS

After the 1919 Chicago riot, civil rights activist Walter White wrote an article in the *Crisis*. The National Association for the Advancement of Colored People (NAACP) publishes this magazine. The NAACP works for equal rights and justice for African Americans. In White's article, he summarized the causes of racial tensions in Chicago. One cause was racial prejudice. White people were prejudiced against black people. There were many other causes. Black workers competed for jobs with white workers. Law enforcement often did not punish white people who committed crimes against black people. Many white people refused to allow black residents to move into their neighborhoods.

all summer. When the raft crossed the line, those tensions turned into violence.

White swimmers threw stones at Williams and his friends. Williams fell off the raft and drowned during the attack. The fighting that followed injured many others. Black swimmers identified the man who they believed had stoned Williams. But the white police officer on duty refused to arrest the man. The incident quickly

White National Guardsmen confront an African American man during the 1919 Chicago race riot.

escalated. By midnight, a full-scale riot had erupted in the South Side neighborhood of Chicago. White rioters targeted this area because many black people lived there.

The riot involved shootings, fistfights, looting, and fires. The National Guard was called in after four days to stop the violence. But fighting continued until August 3.

Then city officials finally regained control of the streets. The effect was devastating. Twenty-three black people and fifteen white people had died. More than 500 people were injured. The destruction left approximately 1,000 people homeless. Most of the victims were African American.

THE GREAT MIGRATION

The riot in Chicago was not an isolated problem. Between May and October 1919, race riots erupted in more than 30 US cities. A race riot is a sudden outbreak of violence motivated by racial hatred. Tensions between white and black people caused these riots. Hundreds of people were killed in the riots. This period of heightened violence was called the Red Summer of 1919.

Thousands of black people moved from the South to the North in the early 1900s. This mass movement was called the Great Migration. Black people fled the South to escape violence, poverty, and discrimination.

But discrimination was also widespread in the North. Many white northerners did not want black people to settle near or in their communities. This attitude created racial tensions.

The Great Migration occurred between 1916 and 1970. During these years, more than 6 million African Americans left the South. Migrants looked for better jobs and cities with less racial discrimination. These waves of migration changed the makeup of US states. In 1900, 93 percent of all African Americans lived in the South. By 1970 that number had fallen to 53 percent.

The Great Migration had lasting effects. Many people who migrated north at this time became

MOVING NORTH

The Great Migration was the nation's largest cross-country migration. Between 1900 and 1910, approximately 200,000 African Americans left the South. Many settled in northern cities, such as New York City. This migration reached its peak in the 1940s. Between 1940 and 1950, 1.45 million African Americans left the South.

MIGRATION PATTERNS

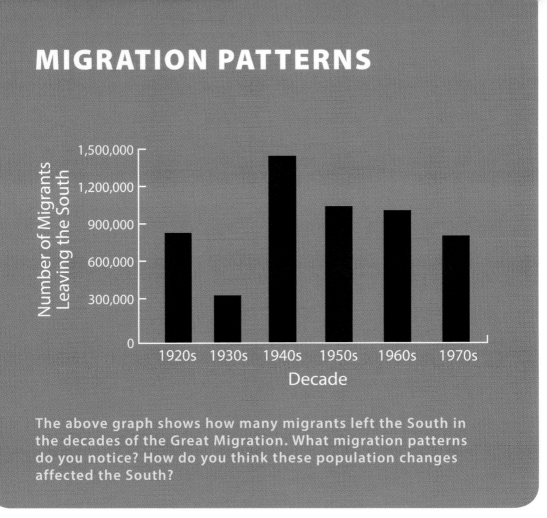

The above graph shows how many migrants left the South in the decades of the Great Migration. What migration patterns do you notice? How do you think these population changes affected the South?

activists and leaders. They fueled the fight for civil rights and equality. The Great Migration's artists inspired new forms of music, painting, and writing. The African American neighborhoods created during the migration shaped cities. Today, historians recognize the Great Migration as one of the nation's most influential and underreported events.

STRAIGHT TO THE
SOURCE

African American author Isabel Wilkerson wrote a book called *The Warmth of Other Suns*. It tells the story of the Great Migration. In an interview, she explained why few people had written about the Great Migration:

> It went on for basically three generations. That meant for any of the journalists who might have been covering it, the ones who started covering it in the beginning weren't there at the end. So it was hard to grasp what was going on.
>
> Another thing is that during the waves of it people kept thinking it was going to end, but the people kept coming. So it was hard to grasp until really after it was over with.
>
> Then finally, people didn't talk about it. . . . [African American families] often didn't tell their children about it. They didn't want to talk about it. It was too painful.

Source: Tavis Smiley. "Author Isabel Wilkerson." *PBS*. Internet Archive, October 7, 2010. Web. Accessed December 11, 2018.

What's the Big Idea?

Take a close look at this text. How does the passage of time affect the way people understand the Great Migration? What reasons does Wilkerson give for why this event has often been overlooked?

CHAPTER TWO

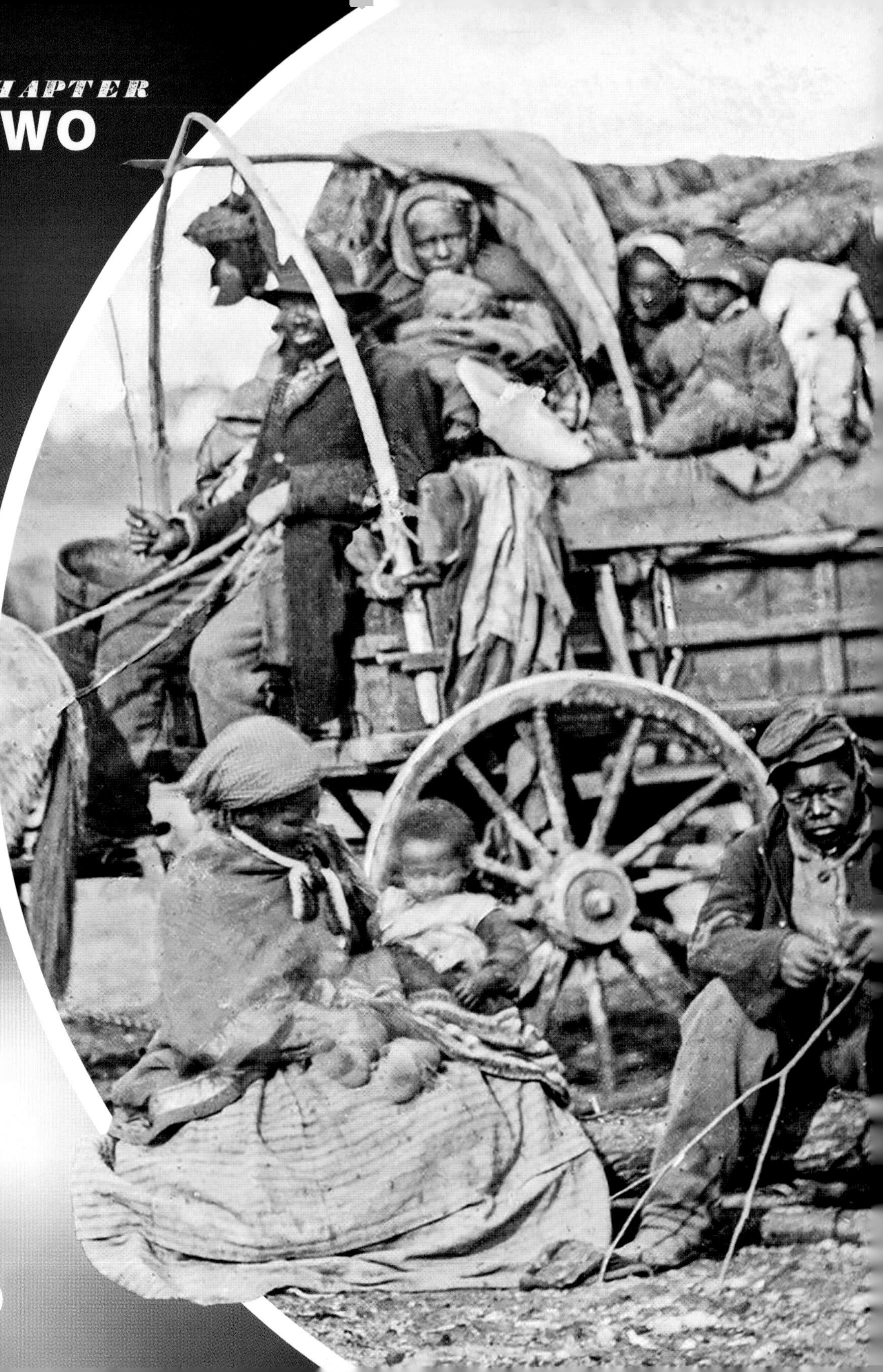

GROWING UNREST

S lavery started the chain of events that led to the Great Migration. The slave trade increased after enslaved Africans were brought to the North American colony of Jamestown, Virginia, in 1619. Some enslaved people were freed after working for a specified period of time. But most remained enslaved their entire lives.

As the United States expanded, so did slavery. By 1860, 4 million people were enslaved in the United States. Most enslaved people worked on plantations in the South. They worked long hours. Many slaveholders beat the people they enslaved. It was legal for

African Americans fled slavery and the South during and after the Civil War.

slaveholders to mistreat their slaves. The law stated that slaves were property, not people.

Slavery was much less common in the North. In some northern states, slavery was outlawed. Many northerners wanted the federal government to outlaw slavery in all states. But many southerners disagreed. They thought each state should make that decision for itself.

This disagreement led to the American Civil War (1861–1865). Eleven southern states formed the Confederacy. Northern states made up the Union. Some border states were also part of the Union. Border states were located between the northern and southern states. They refused to give up slavery. But they did not want to leave the Union.

The Union won the war in 1865. The Thirteenth Amendment was passed in that same year. It freed all enslaved people in the United States.

CONDITIONS IN THE SOUTH

After the Civil War ended, southern lawmakers passed the black codes. These laws allowed white people to continue to control black people. They restricted black people's freedoms. Black people who were unemployed could be arrested and fined. Anyone who could not pay the fine could be forced to work for a period of time without pay.

Black people slowly gained some rights. In the first 12 years after the war, northern leaders rebuilt and governed the South. This period

THE FOURTEENTH AMENDMENT

The Fourteenth Amendment was ratified on July 9, 1868. It granted US citizenship and rights to all people born in the United States. This included people who had formerly been enslaved. But in practice, the amendment was weak. Loopholes allowed for racist practices. For example, courts ruled that it was legal for people to be separated by race as long as facilities for black and white people were equal. But often the facilities provided for black people were worse than those provided for white people.

New schools were created to educate African American children during the Reconstruction period. White and black teachers taught in these schools.

is called the Reconstruction era. In 1870 the Fifteenth Amendment was passed. This amendment gave black men the right to vote. They began to vote in large numbers. Black people could own land and attend school. It appeared as if life would continue to improve for black people.

But the improvements were short-lived. The Reconstruction period ended in 1877.

White southerners regained control of local governments. They began to pass Jim Crow laws. These laws made racial segregation legal. Racial segregation is the forced separation of people into groups based on their races. Black people were forced to use separate services and facilities. They could not attend the same schools as white people. In the 1890s, southern leaders created obstacles that prevented black people from registering to vote. These obstacles included literacy tests and poll taxes. Literacy tests measured a person's reading and writing abilities. These tests were designed to be more difficult for black people than for white people. Many black people could not pass these tests or afford the poll taxes.

Black people also faced employment discrimination in the South. Many employers would not hire them. To make a living, many black people worked as sharecroppers. They grew crops such as cotton on rented land. They paid the landowners with a portion of the crops.

It was nearly impossible for sharecroppers to escape poverty.

Between 1910 and 1920, a bug called the boll weevil ruined cotton crops in the South. The damage caused by boll weevils was devastating for sharecroppers. They earned little money even when harvests were good. The ruined cotton crops left them very poor.

During this time, white hate groups such as the Ku Klux Klan (KKK) began to grow in size. The KKK believes that white people are better than people of other races, especially African Americans. By the 1920s, the KKK had 4 million members across the country. They terrorized and killed African Americans. They used violence to oppress and intimidate black people. These conditions made life difficult and dangerous for black people in the South. This motivated black people to leave the South.

MIGRATION BEGINS

Many black southerners were drawn to the North. They hoped to find more job opportunities in

Black men work at a weapons factory in New York during World War I.

northern cities. These cities were home to many factories. Immigrants normally worked in these factories. But during World War I (1914–1918), government policies slowed immigration to the United States. The unskilled jobs immigrants often took remained unfilled. Many men also left their jobs to fight in the war. Demand for war supplies grew. Businesses needed workers to keep up with the demand. Companies in the North sent agents to the South to recruit workers.

Black migrants in the North wrote to their friends and families in the South. They encouraged their loved ones to move North too. Many southerners were more willing to move if they knew someone in the North. Black newspapers such as the *Chicago Defender* also encouraged people to migrate. The *Chicago Defender* outlined the advantages of living in the North. It featured the success stories of migrants who had made the journey.

FURTHER EVIDENCE

Chapter Two discusses why black people were drawn to the North during the Great Migration. The *Chicago Defender* and other black newspapers encouraged migration. Identify one of the chapter's main points. What evidence is included to support this point? Read the article at the website below. Does the information on the website support this point? Does it present new evidence?

THE *CHICAGO DEFENDER*
abdocorelibrary.com/great-migration

CHAPTER
THREE

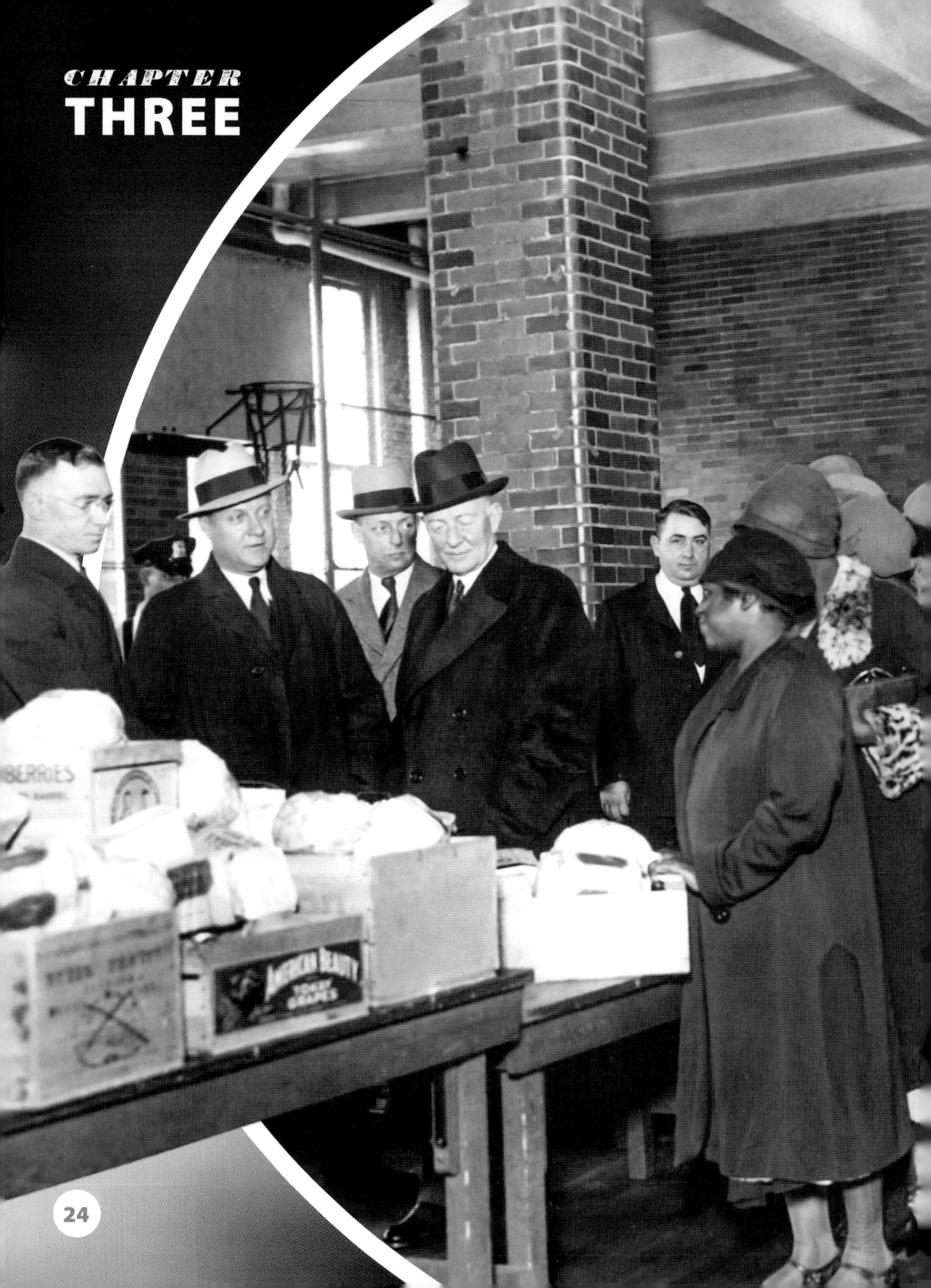

TWO WAVES

Hopes for a better life drew millions of African Americans to the North. The migrants arrived in two major waves. The first wave came between 1914 and 1930. This was the period during and after World War I. Jobs became hard to find in the 1930s. Unemployment spread across the country during this time. This period became known as the Great Depression. Without the promise of work, migration slowed.

The second wave began shortly after World War II (1939–1945) broke out in Europe. The United States wanted to help its allies in the war. Factories increased production of

Unemployed Harlem, New York, residents join a food line during the Great Depression.

weapons and other war supplies. Factory workers were in demand. More jobs became available.

The second wave continued for 30 years. It ended in 1970. By that time, new civil rights laws had been passed. Jim Crow laws were overturned. Civil rights activists had brought about these changes. African American activists fought for equal rights during the American civil rights movement. This movement happened in the 1950s and 1960s. Life improved for black people in the South. The migration of black people to the North again slowed.

TRANSPORTATION

People who wanted to leave the South had several transportation options. The fastest and most direct way north was by train. But train travel was expensive. Early in the first migration wave, northern businesses recruited black southerners and paid for their train tickets. But this did not last long. The cost of tickets kept some people from leaving. Some families had

MAP OF THE MIGRATION

Legend:
- Southwest to Midwest and Far West
- South Central to Midwest
- Southeast to Northeast
- States of Origin

Settlement patterns emerged during the Great Migration. The patterns were loosely based upon train, bus, and highway routes. Do you think these patterns might have been different if more transportation options had been available to black people? Why or why not?

to sell all of their belongings to afford tickets. Other families sent only one family member north. That person earned money and sent it back to the family. When the family had saved up enough money, they moved north.

Migrants faced many obstacles in their journey north. Many had never traveled far from home or taken a train before. Everything was new and strange. Conditions on the trains were poor. Train cars were segregated. Black people could not sit in the same cars as white people. The cars were crowded and dirty. They had no bathrooms. Passengers sat on uncomfortable seats or benches.

Other families traveled by car or bus as far north as their money allowed. Then they stopped and took whatever jobs they could find. After working and saving for a while, they continued traveling north until their money ran out again. They repeated the process several

OBSTACLES

Some white southerners became angry when black people fled the South in large numbers. They relied on the cheap labor African Americans provided. Many white people tried to stop the migration. Sheriffs arrested and fined recruiting agents from the North. They also removed black people from trains headed north. Sometimes police officers arrested groups of black people just so they would miss their trains.

Segregation laws required black people to sit in the back of buses.

times until they reached a place where they wanted

to settle.

CITY LIFE

Most migrants settled in industrial cities in the North.

The populations of large cities such as Chicago and

HOPES AND DREAMS

The documentary *Goin' to Chicago* explores the stories of black migrants who settled in Chicago. African American journalist Vernon Jarrett is one of the people interviewed in the film. Jarrett grew up in Tennessee. He migrated to Chicago in 1946. Like many other migrants, Jarrett had hoped to find a city of peace and equality. Jarrett recalled, "We had great dreams, great fantasies about this place. . . . And of course, much of this was exaggeration. But it was the kind of exaggeration people needed to maintain hope in this country and in their own lives."

Detroit, Michigan, increased. New migrants often moved in with family and friends who had arrived earlier. This settlement pattern resulted in areas where entire communities from the South had re-formed in the North. For example, many black migrants in Chicago came from Mississippi. Some migrants referred to the city as "Mississippi-Chicago."

As more migrants poured into the North, cities could not keep up with the demand for housing. Many white people did not

Children play in Chicago's South Side neighborhood, where most of the city's black residents lived, in the 1940s.

want black people to settle in their neighborhoods. White homeowners often signed special contracts. The contracts said that the homeowners would never sell their home to a black person. This further limited the housing options available to black people.

Black people were forced to live in crowded houses and apartments. They were confined to certain neighborhoods. These neighborhoods were often overcrowded.

Housing was not the only challenge black migrants faced. Many struggled to earn a living. Wages in northern cities were better than wages in the South. But the jobs in the North were still hard. Many businesses only hired migrants for difficult and dangerous work. If a business had to fire workers, the migrants were usually the first to go.

To deal with their hardships, migrants turned to their communities. Migrants supported each other. Black neighborhoods preserved African American cultural traditions. Restaurants served southern comfort foods, such as black-eyed peas and ham hocks. Blues musicians played in nightclubs. These traditions helped make the North feel more like home.

STRAIGHT TO THE
SOURCE

For many migrants, an unknown future in the North was preferable to the violence in the South. In an interview, blues singer Koko Taylor recalled her 1952 journey to Chicago:

> When I was 18 years old, I left Memphis, my husband and I. And we got the Greyhound bus up Highway 61 and headed north to Chicago. He didn't have no money and I didn't have no money. We had one box of Ritz crackers that we split between us. With no money, nowhere to live, no nothing; we was just taking a chance. And I figured, "If he got enough nerve to take a chance with nothin', I have too." So that's what we did.
>
> Source: "Goin' to Chicago." *Media Burn Archive*. Media Burn Archive, n.d. Web. Accessed December 11, 2018.

Consider Your Audience

Adapt this passage for a different audience, such as your friends. Write a blog post conveying this same information for the new audience. How does your post differ from the original text and why?

REFUNDS

TRINITY
TAX SERVICES
GET UP TO
$2000 INSTANT CASH

ADVANCE REFUND LOAN
WHILE YOU WAIT IN 5 MINUTES

NO
SHOOT
ZONE

C
C
PA

THE MIGRATION'S LEGACY

The migration of more than 6 million people changed the racial makeup of many northern cities. Before the Great Migration, few African Americans lived in these cities. African Americans had lived in primarily white neighborhoods. When the flood of migrants began arriving, this changed. Many white residents sold their homes as black people moved into their neighborhoods. This created segregated neighborhoods. Many of these areas remain segregated and poor today. Poor black communities are often

Segregated neighborhoods today still suffer high rates of poverty and violence.

called ghettos. They usually experience higher rates of violence, crime, drug abuse, and poverty. Despite these issues, the Great Migration also left a positive legacy.

THE HARLEM RENAISSANCE

Black artists who came north in the first wave of migrants created a cultural movement. This movement began in Harlem, a neighborhood in New York City. The neighborhood covered only 3 square miles (8 sq km). But it was home to 175,000 African

Americans. It became a magnet for black artists, writers, musicians, and thinkers. The movement they created became known as the Harlem Renaissance.

The Harlem Renaissance lasted from approximately 1918 to 1937. African Americans expressed their experiences through music, art, theater, and writing. These artists sought to create new identities for African Americans. They fought against racism and stereotypes. The Harlem Renaissance was a turning point for black culture. Black people created music, art, and writing that became widely popular. Jazz, an improvised style of music, blossomed during the Harlem Renaissance. Writers such as Zora Neal Hurston, W. E. B. Du Bois, and Alain Locke challenged ideas of what it meant to be black in the United States. Poets such as Langston Hughes created art that reflected black experiences.

MAKING CHANGES

The Great Migration also produced new African American leaders. Many black people were able to

Langston Hughes is famous for poems such as "Let America Be America Again."

vote for the first time when they moved to the North. Voting districts with large black populations elected leaders from their communities to local, state, and national governments. These leaders worked to fix issues that affected many African Americans. Black politicians fought against discrimination. Black activists such as Dorothy Height and Roy Wilkins also joined this fight. One of the most enduring legacies of these leaders is the Civil Rights Act. The US Congress passed this act in 1964. It made racial segregation and discrimination illegal. Many Americans consider it the most important federal law in US history.

In 1965 Congress passed another important civil rights law. It was called the Voting Rights Act. It guaranteed voting rights to all US citizens. It ended laws in the

SLOW IMPROVEMENTS

As new civil rights laws took effect in the 1960s and 1970s, many African Americans saw slow improvements. In 1940, 87 percent of black people lived in poverty. Civil rights laws that ended employment discrimination allowed many black people to earn a better living. Still, it took many decades for meaningful changes to occur. By 2015 the percentage of African Americans living in poverty had shrunk to 25 percent. But many inequalities still exist between white and black Americans. The poverty rate among black people is still much higher today than the poverty rate among white people.

Dorothy Height received a Congressional Gold Medal in 2004 for her work as a civil rights activist.

South that made it difficult for black people to vote. It was a major victory in the fight for equality.

REVERSE MIGRATION

Life in the South became better for black people as civil rights laws were passed. Many people who had migrated north considered returning to the South. Many migrants had family in the South. Businesses had begun to expand there, offering new jobs. Legal segregation had ended.

Some migrants returned to the South. They settled in towns where their relatives had lived. Between 1975 and 1980, more African Americans moved to the South than left it. It was the first time this had happened since the Great Migration began. The trend continued in the following decades. Some people call this trend reverse migration.

The North did not turn out to be the paradise many migrants had hoped for. Black people still faced discrimination and other difficulties there. Yet many found jobs and established communities in the North. They helped bring about lasting changes. Their efforts made the United States a more equal place for all citizens.

EXPLORE ONLINE

Chapter Four discusses the Great Migration's legacy. The website below goes into more depth on this topic. How is the information from the website the same as the information in Chapter Four? What new information did you learn from the website?

THE LONG-LASTING LEGACY OF THE GREAT MIGRATION
abdocorelibrary.com/great-migration

FAST FACTS

- The Great Migration describes the movement of more than 6 million African Americans from southern states to northern states between 1916 and 1970.

- Segregation, violence, a lack of voting rights, and poor wages motivated many black people to leave the South.

- Migrants often settled in cities with other people from their home community. But black people still faced widespread discrimination in the North.

- The Great Migration led to the Harlem Renaissance. This was a cultural movement that began in the mostly black neighborhood of Harlem, New York. African Americans expressed their experiences and created their own identities through art.

- Some migrants became political leaders or activists. They spoke up against discrimination. Their actions helped lead to the passage of the Civil Rights Act and the Voting Rights Act. The Civil Rights Act banned racial discrimination and outlawed segregation. The Voting Rights Act removed obstacles that kept black people from voting.

- Today, inequalities still exist between white and black people in both the North and the South.

STOP AND
THINK

Tell the Tale

Chapter Two of this book discusses what motivated many people to move from the South to the North. Imagine you are living in the South in the early 1900s. Write 200 words about what life in the South is like at that time. In what ways do white people discriminate against black people?

Surprise Me

Chapter Four discusses the Great Migration's legacy. After reading this book, what two or three facts about its legacy did you find most surprising? Write a few sentences about each fact. Why did you find each fact surprising?

Take a Stand

Black migrants faced discrimination and segregation in the North. Many neighborhoods remain segregated today. How do you think politicians and other people can address this problem?

GLOSSARY

colony
land owned by a faraway country or nation

discrimination
the unjust treatment of a person or group based on race or other perceived differences

immigrant
a person who leaves one country to live in another country

migrant
someone who moves from one area to another to seek new opportunities

plantation
a large farm where workers grow crops

prejudice
a feeling of dislike for one person or a group of people because of race or other factors

racism
the belief that certain people are better than others because of their race

segregation
the separation of people of different races or ethnic groups through separate schools and other public spaces

stereotype
a common belief about a group of people that is usually negative and untrue

ONLINE
RESOURCES

To learn more about the Great Migration, visit our free resource websites below.

Visit **abdocorelibrary.com** or scan this QR code for free Common Core resources for teachers and students, including vetted activities, multimedia, and booklinks, for deeper subject comprehension.

Visit **abdobooklinks.com** or scan this QR code for free additional online weblinks for further learning. These links are routinely monitored and updated to provide the most current information available.

LEARN
MORE

Muldoon, Kathleen M. *The Jim Crow Era*. Minneapolis, MN: Abdo Publishing, 2014.

Winter, Max. *The Civil Rights Movement*. Minneapolis, MN: Abdo Publishing, 2014.

ABOUT THE
AUTHORS

Duchess Harris, JD, PhD
Dr. Harris is a professor of American Studies at Macalester College and curator of the Duchess Harris Collection of ABDO books. She is also the coauthor of the titles in the collection, which features popular selections such as *Hidden Human Computers: The Black Women of NASA* and series including News Literacy and Being Female in America.

Before working with ABDO, Dr. Harris authored several other books on the topics of race, culture, and American history. She served as an associate editor for *Litigation News*, the American Bar Association Section of Litigation's quarterly flagship publication, and was the first editor in chief of *Law Raza*, an interactive online journal covering race and the law, published at William Mitchell College of Law. She has earned a PhD in American Studies from the University of Minnesota and a JD from William Mitchell College of Law.

Kate Conley

Kate Conley has been writing nonfiction books for children for more than a decade. When she's not writing, Conley spends her time reading, drawing, and solving crossword puzzles. She lives in Minnesota with her husband and two children.

INDEX